Rev. Jonathan L. Watkins

How to Prepare for a Life of Service

7 Steps to Becoming an

Acts 6 Deacon

"MY MISSION
is to prepare
deacon candidates
for ordination
and
beyond."

WESTBOW
PRESS®
A DIVISION OF THOMAS NELSON
& ZONDERVAN

WestBow Press books may be ordered through booksellers or by contacting:

WestBow Press
A Division of Thomas Nelson & Zondervan
1663 Liberty Drive
Bloomington, IN 47403
www.westbowpress.com
844-714-3454

Because of the dynamic nature of the Internet, any web addresses or links contained in this book may have changed since publication and may no longer be valid. The views expressed in this work are solely those of the author and do not necessarily reflect the views of the publisher, and the publisher hereby disclaims any responsibility for them.

Any people depicted in stock imagery provided by Getty Images are models, and such images are being used for illustrative purposes only. Certain stock imagery © Getty Images.

Scripture quotations marked KJV are from the Holy Bible, King James Version (Authorized Version). First published in 1611. Quoted from the KJV Classic Reference Bible, Copyright © 1983 by The Zondervan Corporation.

ISBN: 979-8-3850-1293-0 (sc)
ISBN: 979-8-3850-1295-4 (hc)
ISBN: 979-8-3850-1294-7 (e)

Library of Congress Control Number: 2023922198

Print information available on the last page.

WestBow Press rev. date: 01/04/2024

Dedication

I dedicate this book to my wife, Kelly Michelle Hendrickson-Watkins. I thank you for your love and support as well as constantly being by my side, praying and encouraging my spirit towards God's destiny for me.

To my mother, the late Mary Alice Watkins of Morristown, New Jersey, for her love and sacrifice as well as instilling in me respect for others, dedication, leadership, community service, and entrepreneurship.

To my daughters, Bianca Michelle Watkins, La'Jon Leigh Watkins, and La'Jean Louise Watkins and my two god-daughters, Tracy Harris and Keva Holman.

Contents

Foreword

The writings and the wisdom the Lord Jesus has given to Pastor Watkins shows his dedication and commitment to the Gospel ministry. We, at the Link Baptist Church, have two young men in training to become deacons, and his book has become the standard bearer. Not only has Pastor Watkins presented the biblical views of God's Word, he has done it with much precision and insight as to how it should be used in a healthy church setting. The church needs to know the meaning and significance of the role of a well-rounded God-fearing deacon. Pastor Watkins has given the world an excellent presentation of the true meaning of the office of deacon. This book encourages as well as instructs about proper protocol of a studied and learned deacon. Pastor Watkins has shown us how to put into practice the love of Christ, the integrity of the scriptures, and the honor of allowing deacons to be used by the Lord and the church. It has been my pleasure and a high honor to suggest this book as a must-read for any and all pastors who truly want and need proper training for the deacons of the church.

This book will give proper insight in understanding the office of deacon. Thank You, Lord Jesus, for using Your manservant to impact the world and the church for the Lord Jesus Christ.

Dr. Kenneth H. McMillan, Pastor of the Link Baptist Church in Macon, Georgia

Acknowledgments

The Late Louise Collins, Marion C. Veasey, Bobby Harper, Mother Hattie Williams, Mother June Clark, Elizabeth Hendrickson-Mason, Rev. Dr. Howard E. Anderson, Rev. Johnnie W. Brewster, Carol J. Sallie, Amy Fletcher, Mother Linda Cody, Robert and Ollie Brister, Perlin "Shuggy" Johnson, Deacon Sylvester Huey.

Thank you to all of those who supported this project:

J.R. Baker-Flowers
Allie Brewster
Natoshia Burney
Lottie Burroughs
Curtis Clemons
Rev. Aaron Clewis
Min. Brian and Kelly Cody
Veronica Collins
William Dawkins
Brandon Demby
Deacon Richard Furell
Willa Hayes

Berma Hicks
Rev. Shantell Hopkins
Rev. Sophia Matthews
Rosemary McCier
Valerie McKenzie
Octavia Muhammad
Freida Nichols
Dr. Normanie Ricks
Sandra Roquemore
Mary Shannon-Nesbitt
Janet Wright
Kishawn Wright

Introduction

7 Steps to Becoming an Acts 6 Deacon was written for people who have been selected by the church to be a deacon, those who are in training to become a deacon, as well as those ordained and currently serving as a deacon. This book gives you an understanding of the different aspects of being a deacon beyond the questions you would be asked during your panel interview before ordination. This book discusses other aspects of being a deacon, which are rarely discussed, like creating a positive relationship with your pastor as well as maintaining a balanced ministry and home life.

Purpose of the Book

Most leadership positions in the church do not have specific formalized training set aside to develop a leader initially, as well as a follow-up to further their understanding of their new or existing position. Opportunities are not provided for continual learning to remain relevant in the ministry and to that local church body. Leadership training should not be a one-time Saturday event, and then you're placed in the position with no additional training or continual mentorship. Training should be ongoing and updated often to not only enhance our leadership skills but to evolve with our ever-changing world. This book will provide you with the training to keep you relevant in your ministry.

The Bible stays the same, but cultures, the views of people, the economy, and technology all change. The church should be aware of those changes and stay relevant to provide a way to salvation discipleship. The depths of our understanding of God changes as we grow closer to Him and become more mature in our faith. Remember, the Word of God stays the same, but the revelation and illumination of those words differ because you look at it through a different set of lenses. When you mature in Christ and have a better understanding of the Bible, God reveals an in-depth understanding of His Word to you.

I have been very fortunate during my career to take advantage of my undergraduate degrees in church leadership and counseling, along with the twenty-eight years in management, before retiring from one of the largest transportation companies in the world, teaching leadership to those new to their position and helping others sharpen their skills to better manage their teams. I have a certification as a growth coach from Dr. Sam Chand's Dream Release leadership program, which has enhanced the leadership of many pastors, assisting them in selecting and managing the right leaders to fulfill the vision God gave to them.

Since 1989, I have taught leadership teams within the church for many different Christian denominations. This training has helped pastors and deacons alike to understand how deacons can help pastors care for the congregation as God intended for them to do. Additionally, I have certifications in human resources and paralegal studies, and I am a P.O.S.T.-certified police chaplain in the state of Georgia, teaching police recruits; these skills enhanced my abilities as a church leader and teacher for pastors, deacons, and lay leaders.

Historically, after the ordination panel interview, the candidates are rarely inspired to go back and discuss the questions to further their education and training as a deacon. Those called to be a minister are licensed and then further their education and training before their ordination as reverend. Most times, you must go to school and obtain a degree before you're ordained as a reverend. Unfortunately, in the role of deacon, those opportunities for additional training are not readily available, because once ordained, you move to the front pew and are assigned leadership tasks that are prayerfully in alignment with your spiritual gifts. It's important that we understand the selection of a deacon, as well as the qualifications for deacons listed in 1 Timothy 3:8–10, 12; 1 Timothy 3:11 states the qualifications for a deacon's wife, which at times are ignored, because the church wants that person as a deacon so much they overlook these biblical requirements. This book will cover seven different areas deacons should cover in their training and keep up to remain effective in their role as a deacon.

My Background

I was fortunate to receive extensive leadership training by the age of sixteen from the late Rev. Dr. Howard E. Anderson, the former pastor of the Greater New Jerusalem Institutional Baptist Church in Morristown, New Jersey. That educational experience was not simply exclusive to me, but to all those young and old who wanted to further their biblical understanding in leadership. My aunt, Marion Veasey, took me to this church because my mother worked on most Sundays until she retired. Aunt Marion helped train me; she was a deaconess at Greater New Jerusalem and taught Sunday school classes.

When I was seventeen, I was in training to become a deacon at First Baptist Church in Madison, New Jersey, where my uncle, Rev. Johnnie W. Brewster, was the pastor. A deacon was required to follow the biblical criteria and had to be twenty-one years of age, as it is their responsibility at times to sign legal documents on behalf of the church. In 1982, I obtained a paralegal certificate from the Institute of Paralegal Studies. In 1983, when I was twenty-one, I was ordained as a deacon. I was licensed to preach the Gospel in 1998 by Rev. S. John Bartley, former pastor of St. John Missionary Baptist Church as well as Journey of Faith Baptist Church in Atlanta. In 1998, I received a BA in Pastoral Counseling from Vision Christian Campus in Lawrenceville, Georgia, and completed a counseling internship at the Gwinnett Regional Youth Detention Center (RYDC). In 2004, he ordained me as a reverend after completing my bachelor of arts in leadership and administration cum laude from Beulah Heights University in Atlanta. I want to offer that same type of training standard to deacons and others coming into the ministry as a leader in the church. I attended the Interdenominational Theological Center in Atlanta for my foundational and preaching studies, then transferred to Louisiana Baptist University towards my master of arts in biblical studies. I obtained a Human Resource Specialist certification from Gwinnett Technical College in Lawrenceville, Georgia. I obtained a Georgia P.O.S.T. certification as a police chaplain and guest lecturer. I completed the Gwinnett County Fire Department and FBI Citizens Academies in Georgia. I retired early with twenty-eight years of service in management in the data center with one of the largest transportation companies in the world, where I obtained certification and experience in program management, conflict resolution, curriculum development, crisis management, and employee development. All of those degrees, certifications, and experiences, as well as others I have obtained over the years, positioned me to look at life through a different lens.

In 1 Timothy 3:13, the King James version states, "For they that have used the office of a Deacon well purchase to themselves a good degree, and great boldness in the faith which is in Christ Jesus." It's important to be an effective leader in the church today, due to the challenging times in the world today. *7 Steps to Becoming an Acts 6 Deacon* gives you a deeper understanding of the position and some aspects of the office of deacon you may not have learned during your training.

It is essential to fellowship with other deacons and those in other leadership positions within the church with like-minded spirits who will walk with you along your journey, while you also motivate them in theirs, as in Proverbs 27:17: "Iron sharpeneth iron; So a man sharpeneth the countenance of his friend." Moreover, this form of ongoing fellowship will aid you in your continual training and thus transform you into a more effective leader and person.

You may ask yourself, *Why do I need to continue my training once I've been ordained as a deacon?* This is a very common question to ask oneself, and I understand. You went through a lot in studying, interviewing in front of a panel of deacons and preachers, standing as the recommendation was read in front of the church, and that glorious day when they laid hands on you. Does that mean you still need ongoing training? The simplest answer is, yes.

The most current and relevant example I will use is when COVID-19 entered the United States, and churches were forced to close their doors. Many deacons and pastors thought closing the physical doors of the church meant ceasing services altogether. Few leaders had the tools or knowledge to pivot from the brick-and-mortar model to the digital space by using social media and other technologies to broadcast the teachings of God. As a deacon, you should be always looking for ways to invest time in making sure you're prepared to fulfill God's vision through different technology streams.

During the pre-ordination process, you come before a council of leaders to interview, but their focus is on the spiritual side of the position. They want to know more about whether you love the Lord, about the different aspects of the church, as well as your understanding of God, and whether you are qualified for the position of deacon. Very seldom is the practical side of the position discussed during your training. The point of this book is to make you aware of the different practical duties of the church you will be responsible for in your position. It's beneficial for you to understand what's needed in the position of a deacon, no matter how long you have served. During our Acts 6 deacon certification training, you will learn all the different aspects of the job and get both a deeper understanding and a hands-on approach in preparation for your ordination and post-ordination.

CHAPTER 1

The Pacesetter

F irst, let's look at the deacon at work.

Some deacons have made great strides to master their leadership skills in ways far beyond their day of ordination. This is very important, because if you don't have a standard to look up to, then how do you know if you are effective in serving God's people in this role? Ask yourself this question: What is the best example of leadership that I can apply to this role?

In Acts 6:5, when the Twelve gathered the disciples together to choose among them seven deacons, "they chose Stephen, a Man full of faith and of the Holy Ghost," and then the disciples named the rest of the seven. It's important that you always look back at those who have been inspirational and effective in their positions as deacons. There had to be something special about Stephen for him to have not only been selected first, but to also have been noted as a man full of faith and the Holy Ghost.

When the church body comes together and prays for direction from the Holy Spirit as they select the deacons God has placed within their congregation, this move of the spirit will enhance the church body, because God knows what's needed for that church and community.

What Does It Take to be The Effective Deacons at Work?

In different periods in my life, I have met some amazing deacons: from an early age, throughout my time of being a deacon until I was ordained a minister, as well as training other deacons over the many years. Now, that's not to say I haven't crossed paths with many ineffective deacons too. As for those who weren't the strongest deacons, I will not linger on them—that would be a distraction from the purpose of this book. I keep these inspirational deacons close to my heart and in my mind often, because they helped frame me as a leader in the church and still inspire me in the present day.

The late Deacon John Elliott was a well-respected man for his depth of faith, wisdom, integrity, and commitment to taking care of his wife and daughter. He always kept a healthy balance between his church and family. He knew how to call on the Lord for guidance, then sit down and reason with people after getting an answer from Him. You may ask what a healthy balance between ministry and family looks like. As a deacon, there are many times when the office may demand you to be at church for meetings with the pastor, leaders, ministries, and members.

However, you must realize that while you work and attend meetings at the church, your spouse or family is home maintaining family life. A deacon must speak up on behalf of himself to ask if all these meetings are necessary as well as productive. Some leaders just like to meet and waste time hearing themselves talk. You notice this when there are more emergency call meetings in between the regularly scheduled meetings. This includes those call meetings right after Sunday service that are supposed to last for fifteen minutes, but turn out to be an hour you cannot reclaim. You will know when those meetings become abusive by the look on the face of your spouse or your children complaining they are hungry and ready to leave. The result of continually calling those meetings can turn your family off from ministry and leadership in the future. The deacons can create a criteria for call meetings, such as limit meetings to one agenda item, limit the duration time of the meeting (after time is expired and a decision cannot be made, the matter should be tabled for another day or the next regular meeting).

The late Deacon Arthur Brown was a straight-talking, successful, business-minded man with a heart for God and God's people. There were times I remember looking up to Deacon Brown due to his tall stature. He would place both his hands on your shoulders, not just in a restful state, but to make sure he had your attention when he spoke truth to you. He would look at you through the bottom of his glasses and say, "We have to do the right thing for the people." In times of decision making in the church, it is important to be reminded that the main focus of the deacon is the greater good of God's people within that community.

When Deacon Robert James first began his training as a deacon, I remember hearing him repeatedly say, "I'm hungry for the Word." Having the type of spirit that hungers and thirsts after Christ will keep you not only humble, but also focused on being an effective deacon. Deacon James is a chef by trade, and he uses those opportunities to share the goodness of Christ while serving you. I've seen Deacon James witness to people while carving or serving portions of meat. Can you image Deacon James coming over to you with his big smile while you are eating and inviting you to Christ?

Deacon Stan Reeves is a utility deacon. Reeves knows and loves the Lord, and he can teach, offer sound advice, and sing, as well as being well known in the community. He is dedicated to serving the pastor and people. He is one of few who can stay relevant and effective as well as have the respect of all. Deacon Reeves often carries the weight of the ministry on his shoulders and knows how to call on the Lord for help before making decisions. His knowledge of the community is an asset when the pastor and people need assistance or resources. His love of his community goes as far as being an Atlanta Falcons, Hawks and Braves fan, but I don't hold that against him. The closes I come is being fans of the WNBA Atlanta Dream.

Deacon Larry Ruff knows how to get heaven's attention through his prayers. As a deacon, you need to know how to go to God in prayer on a continual basis, as Moses did while in the wilderness. Moses spent a lot of time talking to God for guidance on handling the people as well as direction to lead them. Deacon Ruff's humble spirit is also very inviting to a sinner who wants to learn more about Christ. It's a special kind of person who knows how to call upon God on behalf of others and display a fun spirit.

Deacon Richard Furell's dedication to God and his respect for God's servant, his pastor, and the church have always been outstanding. As the chairman of the board, he works well with all ministries, assisting them as needed to minimize murmuring. He makes sure the building is maintained inside and out for service each week, which takes the stress off any pastor. His hunger for learning more about God and how he can be more effective in his ministry is a standard every deacon should strive for as a leader. Not only has he opened his heart to God, to his training, and to servitude, but he often opens his family's home and swimming pool for baptisms.

Deacon Enoch Ford expresses his faith through song. This brother's singing makes you preach harder than you would have ever prepared to in your preaching manuscript, because the Holy Spirit is in your midst to give you the words needed to answer the prayers of the people. It is his relationship with God that allows him to execute his songs with such passion and inspiration. Those of us who have the gift of singing know the importance of ushering in the Holy Spirit during a service. There are times when the spirit is heavy in the church due to the life of a Christian, and that song from a deacon can ease the heaviness. As a deacon, I have been called upon to sing and have asked deacons to sing before I preach to invoke the Holy Spirit in the service.

The late Deacon Joseph Allen also expressed his faith through song. Very few singers can truly move listeners instead of just trying to invoke an emotional catharsis each Sunday for the congregation. Deacon Allen was inquisitive about learning more about the Lord. He would ask questions about certain scriptures and life.

His big heart was shadowed by his shyness, which made him very humble as a leader in the church.

Deacon Leonard Blackshear is always full of love. This brother has one of the most humbling spirits I've ever seen. No matter what situation he is placed in, he is never boisterous or overbearing towards others just to prove his point.

His voice is smooth, but his words are so strong and effective when he ministers. This is the kind of spirit that will calm any soul in crisis. It's like having a person who knows the Word of God speak to you in a calming voice when others are loud and erratic. This type of deacon can be very effective in a church meeting, family meeting, or relationship meeting. Can you imagine someone giving homage to you not because of the position you held, but because of the impact you made on their lives? Be the best you can be as you continue your training, in addition to pre- and post-ordination.

Who are the deacons I looked up to in earlier years, compared to some of the leaders in the church today? Listed below are some men who loved God and served their pastors and the church well, without hesitation, although for some reason, they were not selected for ordination:

(1) Brother Dexter Holmes (Preaching Help). Every pastor could use that deacon who truly encourages you while you are preaching, just to affirm what you are saying is true, encouraging, and meaningful to change the lives of God's people through His Word. I'm not talking about the deacon who shouts, "Amen!" to

everything the preacher says, from hello to good-bye. Deacon Holmes heard me preach for the first time after attending several of my Bible studies, and he shouted, "Put your weight on it, Pastor." I thought he was talking about my physical weight, because we both were big guys, but he meant to continue to stand flat-footed and preach the Gospel as an encouragement not only on Sunday morning, but for a lifetime.

(2) Brother Wayne Diggs (Encouraging). Brother Diggs was what my family called him. He was not a deacon, but an usher and close brother at the church. I was ordained as a minister, and Brother Diggs was the type of silent leader and stakeholder. The kids could not get away with anything in church (and neither could the adults) because he knew how to talk to you while pushing up his glasses with his finger. This type of person is needed more in the body of Christ for our youth. Imagine children misbehaving, and Brother Diggs walks in and gives them the look. The respect he generated when they corrected their actions is truly missed today.

(3) Brother Willie Hawk is a retired Naval officer who came to give his knowledge, leadership, and passion to the church. Not only did he serve in a ministry, but he also took on many other active roles within the church. He served as chairman of the Church Board of Trustees and assumed responsibility for the maintenance and upkeep of the stressed facilities and grounds. Brother Hawk procured chairs, desks, refrigerators, lawnmowers, and other much-needed equipment for the church. Whether it was painting, carpet installation, plumbing, or changing light bulbs, there wasn't a job that was too large or too small for him. This brother worked tirelessly to ensure the sanctuary, classrooms, and Fellowship Hall were in proper repair and ready for ministry. He also regularly attended Bible study, wanting to learn more about the Gospel. He would give

me that inquisitive look when I taught Bible study, which let me know he wanted to know more, and that prompted me to circle back around in the lesson and provide more information for him and the others. His experience, leadership, and commonsense approach made him a valued confidant and a great sounding board. He was able to encourage me and others to help him because of the spirit in which he was using his gifts. Some church members charge the church the same price for their labor as they would a new client. Alternatively, some churches have a habit of abusing the gift of members by overloading them with projects for free.

There are deacons in the church, retired or not, who have a lot to offer with their gifts and talents, but pastors and church members must get to know the deacons and allow them to use their gifts, because God will add to the church what's needed for the ministry in that community.

(4) Brother Brandon Demby is a high school teacher in Gwinnett County, Georgia, who has made quite an impact on the lives of religious leaders and children. The gifting that has been given to him by God places him in a position to make an immediate impact on those he meets. He is a five-star chef who teaches students how to cook, and during his classes, he also shares life lessons. Students are encouraged to make the right decision in life as well as cope in this ever-changing world. The students call him "Chef," but I call him "Deacon"; he's always been willing to serve through his encouraging words to me over the years. He teaches preparation and presentation of food, and he also has a green thumb; yes, a green thumb. He has shown his work both within the church and at my home. This brother still asks questions or texts his thoughts on the Bible, looking for additional knowledge. It's important to spend

time with members to get to know them and, through the gift of discernment, encourage them in the direction God would have them to be a blessing to the church and the community.

What Did They Offer Compared to Deacons Today?

The earlier deacons utilized their personality; they utilized their gifts, talents, and skills. They brought what they had to the church and offered it as a sacrifice to God. The gifts God gave them made them more effective in their duties. Earlier deacons used their gifts, unlike the way some are trained today. The current structure of leadership training doesn't always encourage those gifts or skills. There should be a process during new members orientation to learn more about the person God sent to your church. Also, there should be another process to onboard their gifts and talents into the church ministries.

For example, deacons who have the gift of singing, encouraging, or praying should be allowed to exercise those gifts and others. There are times when pastors need someone to pray with them, encourage them, offer them wise counsel, or sing during the service to lift their spirit and help focus their mind on the service before they preach God's word. Dr. Martin Luther King often had Mahalia Jackson sing before he preached. As a pastor, can you imagine having a person with that inspiring talent on your Deacon Board or in your church or your phone contacts you could call to help you? Those are the people you want to receive the best ongoing training.

My uncle, the late Pastor Johnnie W. Brewster, and I would go to the room on the side of the pulpit to discuss issues and concerns during the service before he preached, which I now call the "back room talk." No one knew what we discussed in that back room, but we came out with a plan after prayer. Why is this important in the life of a pastor? At times, people think the pastor is a dumping ground for all of their personal problems, the church's problems and the community's concerns. Pastors need someone to talk with freely and confidentially. Deacons also need someone to go to for encouragement and wise counsel.

The Perception of the Office

Many people seem to think deacons should control the pastor or the church body, ensuring that everything runs according to the vision of the Deacon Board and stakeholders, versus the vision of God through the pastor. That improper mindset causes confusion in the church body. It also causes disdain and division in the leadership of the church, even though we are supposed to follow 1 Corinthians 12:12, which states, "For as the body is one and hath many members, and all the members of that one body, being many, are one body, so also is Christ."

Leaders of the church should not only be aware of this, but pray and ask God to remove that type of negative spirit from the body of Christ within the leadership team of the church. I've consulted many pastors, and through my discernment, I found some ineffective leaders who should be reassigned to nonleadership tasks. I find this type of negative spirit also when the church is without a pastor for a period of time. When they're in search of a new pastor, much prayer, discernment, and cooperation are needed within the church body. When the office of pastor is vacant (and there's no assistant pastor), the chairman of the Deacon Board is essentially the next leader of the church, and that can be a challenging position for any deacon. Challenges occur because few deacons have the opportunity to lead a church without a pastor.

Many preachers will just show up to the church with their resume in their hand; there will be calls from other church pastors wanting to place their choice on the list, so be prepared. When this happens, you must work closely together with the Deacon Board and pastoral search committee, so those on the outside of the church can see you all are working together as one body through this process.

If you are a team of deacons, leaders within the church working together to fill that vacant position, then the transition is effortless as you follow the guidance of the Holy Spirit. To support you through that process, I created an interviewing guide that minimizes any human resources issue, such as asking personal or inappropriate questions of candidates.

The guide contains a variety of in-depth questions. For more information, I invite you to reach out to us at www.JLWattsEnterprise.com.

The selection of a deacon at times is based on the strongest voice in the church, the one who consistently gave the most money in the offering plate, the one who had a business in the community, or just one of the older members. When you really look at those characteristics and how some churches select a deacon based on those qualifiers, this actually works against the church spiritually, because they were not of honest rapport, full of the Holy Ghost and wisdom. Please note just because a person is well into their senior years of life doesn't mean they automatically have wisdom. On the flip side, just because you don't qualify for a senior meal doesn't necessarily mean you don't have wisdom. It would be better if the church followed the scripture in Acts 6:3, which lists the characteristics for a deacon, rather than create their own. In any leadership position, you always want the perception to be positive among the membership—a positive experience for anyone who is in the position or becomes your successor in that position. The deacon in the church was always looked upon as a great leader, a highly elevated position in the church next to the pastor, due to their ordination by the laying of the hands on them.

When I was a deacon, my uncle sent me to join the Deacon's Union. On a monthly basis, deacons from different churches would gather together and discuss various aspects of the position of a deacon. Oftentimes, some deacons had issues or concerns that were going on in their church, and they were able to express it there and receive positive feedback as well as guidance on how to handle it based on others who came through that issue. This type of union was very positive with the pastors because they knew the deacons were not getting together to plot against them, but to help enhance the church body as a whole. The deacons who were members of that union were from several different churches over the cities in New Jersey. Even now, I still hold my union card to show I was a member of the Deacon's Union. When you complete our deacon certification training in preparation to be ordained, we offer you the option to become a monthly member. The membership program is open to all deacons. In addition, on a quarterly basis, we offer classes for deacons on different subjects to help them with their continuing education and training. To become a part of this monthly membership program, you don't have to be an ordained deacon. You could be in training to be a deacon. Oftentimes, our churches don't have someone to offer these types of training, and pastors are often too busy to stop and train all the leaders in the church. My company, JL Watts Enterprise LLC, provides leadership training for busy pastors. Our motto is "We Help Define, Develop, Disciple" leaders.

The Reality of the Office

The reality of the office is that the deacon is there to assist the pastor with the responsibility of taking care of the concerns of the church membership. If you remember, back in Acts 6:1, the numbers of followers had multiplied, and the Grecians began murmuring against the Hebrews, because the widows were being neglected. How is that text applied to the present tense? We have social services that perform those duties as well as government agencies that provide assistance, so why do you need a well-trained deacon today?

The title of this book mentions Acts 6, because despite the very essence of what that position was created for, there lies the harsh reality that people today are still being neglected. The deacon can only try to make sure that the membership is satisfied to the point where there are no uproars; if there's no division or infractions within the church body, then they've done a great job as hard as it is. How is this accomplished?

Little sparks of fire are often observed within the church, and it's important to manage those small fires immediately before they become an uncontrollable blaze. When it comes to uproars in the church, the deacon can be effective in bringing a calm to the situation. First, after much prayer, eliminate rumors in the church among the leadership by being on the same page when addressing others, which minimizes the congregation from perpetuating the rumors. If you don't know by now, when a situation arises in the church, the members usually call their deacons and church leaders for confirmation, more information, as well as direction. Second, deacons can minimize divisions by supporting the pastor and their Godly vision. If, through prayer and a strong cohesive leadership team, the membership can come together to follow the vision and plan that God has for that church and community, then you will see unity. Lastly, deacons can minimize infractions by being of one accord as leaders, moving in the same direction, stepping to the same beat of the drums, showing the church and community that their faith in God will see them through all adversities.

Many leaders don't have the people skills or personality to manage differences of opinions and crises, as well as the removal of bad leadership in the church. Have you ever worked with an irritating person at your job, and everybody knew that person didn't perform their job well and others always had to help carry their load? Everyone complained at one time or another, good people quit, but management never did anything about it. The same goes on in the church, because that same person got themselves a leadership position in the church, and maybe on stage every Sunday, but the pastor didn't remove them. However, good ministry workers stepped down and maybe even left the church, but the pastor made no attempt to remove the ineffective leaders. The one rotten negative spirit will affect the whole body of the church.

Deacons and leaders in the church who are ineffective cause problems, and that's why you see so many issues and so many divisions. Many infractions in the church are because the leadership is not maintaining cohesiveness in a spiritual way. It's because there's not a lot of praying, there's not a lot of supplication, there's no ongoing training or a place for deacons to discuss their concerns, and there are not many teams working together as one body in Christ. For example, if leaders had crisis training, they would know how to handle situations that arise within the body of the church. If the deacons had a meeting with other like-minded deacons and discussed church issues and concerns without blaming the pastor and other leaders, and they receive positive spiritual feedback, those deacons could go back to their respective churches armed with better skills to implement. Those skills can include communication and knowing how to listen more than speak. Classes in anger management help people work through problems by teaching others individually or in groups, which would be a big impact on ministries having problems.

Continual education will inspire leaders to stay relevant and be effective in their church.

The leaders—whether within the church or the community—who have fulfilled their duties well should be honored by our actions and through our remembrance of them. When you can envision yourself within their leadership style and effectiveness in the church and within your community, then you know you're on the right path to fulfilling your position. To assist you, find a mentor you can learn from as well as enhance your leadership skills. It's important to have a coach or mentor you can look up to, who can help develop your skills. There were several men and women over the years who fulfilled that role for me.

Please understand, when striving for excellence, you have to be coachable to the point that you are prepared to change to better yourself in your position. This means a deep level of transparency to those challenges identified within you. God knew Moses had challenges speaking before Moses admitted it to Him at the burning bush. Yet, God still used him, as well as many other men and women in the Bible who had challenges.

Mentors and coaches for pastors, deacons, and church leaders can be obtained through JL Watts Enterprise's website, www. JLWattsEnterprise.com. It is imperative to have an open mind and a willing spirit to not only continue your growth in your position, but to know that there is help available to you.

CHAPTER 2

The Profile

It is important that you get an idea of what the deacons look like in different aspects of their life. When I was first set aside as a deacon, I was seventeen years old. I had an understanding of what a deacon should look like or a standard of what a deacon should be at a very young age, because I grew up in a teaching church. The late Rev. Dr. Howard E. Anderson was the pastor of Greater New Jerusalem Institutional Baptist Church in Morristown, New Jersey. He was not only a teacher in the public school system, but a professor at the Northern Baptist School of Religion in Newark, New Jersey. He made sure that each and every one of his members knew our positions as associate ministers, deacons, trustees, teachers, and ministry leaders. It didn't matter if you were young, middle-aged, or a senior; he was willing to teach you if you were willing to learn. People would come from near and very far to attend his training and get an opportunity to serve on Sundays. After being in that church, I understood all the different positions in ministry, from the pulpit to the front door as an usher; I was more effective when I started attending my uncle's church and could work in different capacities efficiently, except for playing the Hammond organ and preaching God's Word. My acceptance to my calling to the ministry came much later in life.

I had the pleasure of working with the late Deacon Homer Waddell, who took time with the youth to show us various aspects of church work. He had us meet him on Saturdays to help him clean the church; we didn't know he was teaching us how to be positive young men, as well as understand how to take responsibility for caring for the church property. Teaching us to care for the church property subsequently, in a subliminal way, taught us how to care for our own home. We would take pride in cleaning around the outside of our house and the neighborhood.

Deacon Waddell worked at Roots Men's Clothing Store in Morristown, New Jersey. He taught us as young men how to dress, match our clothes, and tie our ties. Matching our tie and shirt along with our suit is a seemingly lost art, because of the direction in which fashion has evolved. He taught us deacons should always present themselves well-dressed in public, as well as at the church.

We also had the late Deacon Valentine Baker at the church, who was a very skillful mason; one time, he came over to our house and built a cement retaining wall in front of it due to a hill of dirt sliding down and weakening the front part of the lawn. While helping him work on the retaining wall, we talked about many subjects. He was from the Islands and shared some of his past, which included sharing his life skills as a man.

Those two gentlemen, Waddell and Baker, showed me a standard of what a deacon should be, in the home, in the church, in the community, and in my professional life.

In the home, the deacon should be the head of the house in providing love towards his spouse and family. This love is not just shown on special occasions like birthdays, anniversaries, and holidays, but on a consistent basis.

In the church, the deacon should be seen as a leader working together with the pastor, other church leaders, and members. The deacon should not be seen as a patsy or yes-man for the pastor. Respect flows both ways when the pastor and deacons focus on fulfilling God's will for the church and community.

In the community, the deacon should be seen as a representative of God and the church. The deacon should have community resources that benefit the church as needed in a positive way. For example: if a family is in need of food and the church can't help, then the deacon should be aware of a local food bank he could direct that family to. The deacon should be aware of agencies like the United Way.

In their professional life, deacons should maintain a job as well as display the same character on Sunday as during the week, which shows they are not two-faced, but actually live what they teach.

This is important if you want to be the best in your position as an Acts 6 deacon. Remember, none us are perfect, but we should strive to be like Jesus. When we stumble and sin, we should ask for forgiveness and strive to do better.

What Does a Deacon Look Like?

In the Home

You may ask yourself what a deacon looks like in the home. A deacon should be of the same temperament in the church as at home. If you can't take care of your home and family, showing them love and respect, then how can you effectively take care of the membership of the church? So many aspects of family life, which you can try to achieve as best you can in a loving way, will carry over directly into the church. If you're at home and arguing all the time or keep your family upset by constantly creating confusion within the home, you will undoubtedly bring that same toxic mindset with you into the church. Being a leader of the church, you must be able to maintain an even temperament in the church and home.

There should be a separation when it comes to sharing information from the church. For example, concerns talked about during the board or official staff meetings are not to be discussed at home. Sharing information from meetings is how personal information of members get out among the members. For example, if the board discussed assisting a family with housing, it can be embarrassing to the family in need. Agenda items shared with the congregation can be misunderstood, because the person sharing the information inappropriately didn't understand all the facts or wanted to sway the vote their way.

Additionally, you cannot and should not bring things from your pastor's, deacon's, and leadership meetings home to your family. There are times when you're going to be stressed out with the different situations that happen in the church, related to business, or even stressed out because you couldn't help a family with some of the trials and tribulations they are experiencing financially, physically, mentally, or even emotionally. When it comes to your home, there has to be some sanctity and boundaries put in place. It has to be a place where you can rest and have peace of mind. If your home is not a place where you can do that, where you create a balanced separation, then it makes it very hard for you to be an effective deacon or leader. Have you ever talked about someone from work so much, when your spouse finally meets them for the first time, they give that person an evil look before they greet them? This happens within the church too.

I think about the late Deacon John Elliott, who took care of his wife, who was ill, and had a daughter in college. He also maintained his position as chairman of the Deacon Board. He did all that, because he knew how to separate one from another. He didn't bring home the worries of the church to his family. He didn't bring the worries of his family to the church. He understood the balance of home and church was so important to keep separate.

In the Church

When it comes to the church, the deacon has to be looked upon as one of its leaders. The deacon has to be viewed as a go-to person for information, resources, and various spiritual guidance in the church. I will never forget Deacon Stan Reeves, who was one of very few people members always went to with questions, as well as help with different resources. He worked for the United States Post Office, and he knew all the different places around Atlanta. He knew where to eat, where to go for social programs, and who the important people were (or someone who could go to that important person). He stayed in contact with different people he met, whether through his job on a route or conversation at an event. He always kept that information readily available to reach back out and extend to another family, as well as share with the deacons and the pastor.

Deacon Stan Reeves, Deacon Ronald Fuller, and Deacon Reggie Fuller would stop by the church on their lunchtime or after work to handle different matters, because they were very resourceful and skilled, and could fix almost anything. The deacon in the church has to be someone the congregation can trust to go to for help, as well as the pastor too.

The deacon should also be a resource for the pastor, especially if he doesn't live in the community where the church is located; he may not know the important contacts and agencies and people needed for the church to be relevant. A deacon has to be of honest rapport, full of the Holy Ghost and wisdom, because that's the biblical requirement for that position. If you're fulfilling those aspects of your position in the church, you are doing a great service. If you have not yet fulfilled those aspects, continue reading this book, and you'll find out more information on how to better yourself in those areas of what an Acts 6 deacon should be like in the church.

In the Workplace

The deacon in the workplace is another area of great importance. If you're already ordained or have been selected to become a deacon, this is where people see you most. This is where the workplace environment becomes so important in the life of a deacon. Why do I say that? You interact with more people during your workday than at church and sometimes at home. How many times have you seen people at work behaving crazy, cursing, hollering, screaming, throwing stuff, having tantrums, talking down to people, not following directions of their management staff, and yet, they claim they are Christians? Isn't your first question to those people, *What church do you go to?* even if you say it in your head. You asked that question because you want to make sure you don't go to that church, because there may be more people like that at that church, who call themselves leaders. They see you at your most vulnerable points at work.

The workplace is where potential members as well as those who don't know the Lord actually see how you handle stress, how you handle anger, how you handle adversity, and how you handle different situations that impact the flow of your daily work. Are you a go-getter on the job? Are you the type of person who will help others move ahead? Are you a lazy person? Do you come to work late and half work, don't fill your portion of the job, leaving it for someone else? Are you a person others can go to when they're struggling, when they're trying to make it? Do you receive low evaluations? Are you someone who goes for extra training to better understand your job? Are you the person management goes to first and asks questions, because they value your insight? Are you that person that when things get rough, when things get tough, when someone feels like quitting, they come to you for wise counsel? Do they come to you for encouragement, for a way out of a problem? Do they come to you for godly advice? Are you the type of person people go to when things get bad? Why? Because you have the spirit of God within you and wisdom enough to know what to say and how to say it after seeking counsel from God.

Are you that fun person at work who everybody likes to be around? When things are down at work, can you ignite the team? Are you that person who can get the team together and fill the quota or finish the project? Being that type of person at work is so effective, because if you can do it at work, and they see you walk like Christ at work of honest rapport, full of the Holy Ghost and wisdom, if they can see your integrity at work, they will follow you, because of the Christ that's within you, not just because you're a great speaker, not just because you're a great person. Are you that type of person? Moreover, would you want to become that type of person? If so, let's get you registered into our certification training.

In the Community

I had the pleasure of working with Deacon Mark Smith, who was a counselor with a great ability to connect with people right where they were in their life. His gift of teaching group classes drew people to the church. One of the requirements he made was there had to be some type of anonymity within the church of those who attended the empowering group sessions. Once those people were able to come to their meetings and feel comfortable sharing, the church made an impact on that community. The church scheduled the meetings on a night where attendance was very low and where there wouldn't be a lot of people meeting. Deacon Smith was the type of guy who was rigid and straightforward, even while singing, but he was also very funny. This guy had so many jokes. He would make you laugh for hours. Most of all, he knew Christ and loved the Lord, because he knew God changed him into a person who could help someone else, who could uplift anyone out of their situation, and who his family could be proud of, because of the God that's within him.

You will hear me say this throughout this book: The God within you enables you to go forth and be effective in ministry. And that's why I often refer to the selection of a deacon in Acts 6:3, where it states, "Of honest report, full of the Holy Ghost and wisdom." Those are the attributes of Christ within you that make you a deacon. I mean, leaders have it, different people have it, but you must possess it, because you were selected from those attributes for the church to fulfill a need. Those who don't possess those characteristics can deceive the members. You were set aside for this office, and because you were selected and set aside for this office, it's your obligation to keep up with your training. Can you imagine having a deacon in your church who is community-minded and has the heart of the people? What an impact that would have on the ministry and its people to have someone teaching entrepreneurial classes, financial literacy, wills, trusts, credit repair, coping with mental health, and so on. There are many community agencies that can't afford their own brick-and-mortar, but would be glad to partner with your church for some space.

CHAPTER 3

The Purpose

People often overlook Acts 6:1–8 in reference to the selection of a deacon. Many times, we look at Timothy 3:8–9, referencing those five characteristics as the only qualifications for a deacon. We should not disregard those qualifications, but we should make sure we understand the selection process of the office first. If you are not of honest report and full of the Holy Ghost and wisdom, then you were not even considered for the office. Once we understand the selection process, then we can go to 1 Timothy 3:8–9. We should uphold those different characteristics of a deacon: be grave, not double-tongued, not given to much wine, not greedy for filthy lucre, holding the mystery of the faith in a pure conscience. It's expected that both of those scriptures go hand-in-hand to fulfill the office of a deacon. In our Acts 6 deacon certification training, we make sure you understand both aspects of the selection process and the qualifications of a deacon before your ordination.

Why Were Deacons Needed in Acts 6?

Complaining

The reason why deacons were selected in the early church was that the number of disciples had multiplied, and there were murmurings among the Grecians against the Hebrews about their widows being neglected. Growth in the church will happen in the life of any ministry, which is the goal to grow the church through discipleship by reaching out to those who have not yet accepted Christ as their personal Savior. During this evangelistic ministry, there will be some murmuring, uneasiness, unrest, anger, and resentment between the initial members, existing members, and the newer members. Some call this a culture war within the church. Some churches try to appease the different cultures by having a contemporary service at the morning service, traditional service at 11:00 a.m., and maybe a youth service in the afternoon. Deacons can close the gap between the members by encouraging both cultures to work together on ministries. It would be an advantage to have representation of both cultures on the Deacon Board, once again showing the membership how to work together in the church with the focus of helping the community.

Older members may look at the life of the ministry through a dated set of lenses, which was effective at the inception of the church. However, changes in life are inevitable, and the church leader's approach to these changes is key to keeping the church alive. The existing members don't always have an open mindset; they may not be welcoming towards new people coming into the church if they think the culture may change. New pastors go through this more often. Sometimes, this happens between the young and the senior members or when you have mixed cultures. It all depends on who was at the church first; they may have dug in and are set in their ways and resist different processes and procedures of the church. As a church consultant and coach for pastors, I run into this culture tug-of-war when processes and procedures need to be updated or removed. A new vision, ineffective leadership, revised federal or state laws, and technology changes are driving forces for culture changes.

Another aspect we are teaching in our training towards certification of becoming an Acts Chapter 6 deacon is knowing about the different resources in your community that can support your members. The church is very important and vital to the life of your community. Not all churches have the finances or resources to help their members, so you reach out into the community for small or even large resources. When I was teaching on Monday nights in a church in southwest Atlanta, people would often knock on the door and ask for assistance, because we were a church that was open at night in that community. We didn't have the assistance they needed at the church, but I would connect them with the United Way by dialing 211, and most times, they got the help they needed. Simply knowing who to call at the right time when someone needs it shows your level of interest in the membership for their welfare and their well-being.

Compassion

When it comes to compassion by the deacon, that aspect of your duty is guided by the Holy Spirit. When people come to the deacon, and they're in mourning, or they have an emotional problem or a medical situation, your compassion and empathy shows them you care for them, even in the midst of their time of need. Since 1998, I've served as a police chaplain with the Gwinnett County, Georgia, police department. I've come across many different instances where families are stranded, in mourning, in crisis, or in need of social services, and just knowing who to call was effective. I didn't have a utility belt with all the answers for their particular needs, but I did possess the Holy Spirit to guide me; I also had the resources on my phone to help me get them what they need.

When we don't reach out to the community or interact with them, we lose out on different aspects of our job as deacons; some churches expect the community to run into their buildings, but we show compassion by reaching out to those in need and obtaining different resources for them. We have a 501c3 nonprofit program that collects items like toiletries, blankets, socks, and beanies, to name a few. We take those items, place them into a backpack, and give them to police officers to carry in their trunks. When they identify a homeless person or family in need, the officer gives them the items in the backpack. This is community work that can be done by the deacon as a church project. For more information on the 501c3, I invite you to reach out to us at www.JLWattsEnterprise.com.

Commitment

When it comes to commitment as a deacon, it's not about you; it's about assisting the pastor to fulfill God's vision for the church. The commitment comes in when you are taking care of the needs of the people, while the pastor focuses on the Word of God. This doesn't mean being a yes-man, nor does it mean being the devil's advocate every time the pastor proposes something in a meeting. It does mean you will allow the Holy Spirit to guide you in your duties, being honest in your talk and your walk by saying what you mean and meaning what you say at all times, in a loving way, so the one you are talking to will receive it.

When Kelly, my wife, was in school, I was the interim pastor and promised a young girl in our church that I would attend her school recital. After I had preached that morning, my family and I went to get something to eat before her recital. While we ate, Kelly was doing her homework, but she was taking so long I was afraid we'd be late. All I could think about was the young lady looking out into the crowd and not seeing us in the audience, after I had promised to be there. The later it got, the more anxious I became, trying to remain cool while hurrying Kelly along.

I remained calm as long as I could, but it got so late to the point where I said, "Hey, we need to go."

I wanted to be able to sit where the young girl could see us. Children hold you accountable when you make a commitment to them, as a leader and as a parent. After Kelly finished her homework, we went to the community center, where the recital was being held. We arrived at the center, and one of the associate ministers was out front; he said he'd guide us to our seats. I had hoped he would save us some seats, but there were five in my group, so I didn't expect to have a front-row seat. I was willing to stand in the back so she'd be able to at least see we were there.

I walked down the hall, and he kept saying, "Come on, go this way, go this way. It's right in here."

I got to the door, opened it, and walked in, and everyone said, "Happy birthday." What a relief that we weren't late, because it was a surprise birthday party they set up, but the point is, I didn't want to disappoint the young lady and her family by not attending her recital. It was a great surprise to me, and we had a great time. It's important not to make a promise, because due to circumstances, you may not make every event.

I was grateful that Pastor Joe L. Spann Jr. gave me the opportunity to be the interim pastor and grateful to the members of Fully Rely On God Christian Ministry in Douglasville, Georgia, for celebrating my birthday.

Communion

Communion deals with the relationship between the people and Jesus Christ. It's important to know we should commune with one another and create relationships as Jesus did, reaching people right where they are in life. The disciples asked the people to look among them and find seven men of honest report, full of the Holy Ghost and wisdom. In doing this, they were able to commune with one another, collaborate, and pick seven men.

The Bible names the seven men they picked, and one was Stephen, a man full of faith and the Holy Ghost. One of the ordinances in the church is communion, which is handled by the deacons. In some churches, the deaconess prepares the sacrament, and the deacons distribute it at the direction of the pastor. Being a deacon in the church of honest report reminds me of when I would leave my uncle's church and go to the church down the street and help them out from time to time. I enjoyed their service and had many friends who attended that church.

One time, someone told me, "I like when you come to our church to serve communion; please make sure you try to make it every first Sunday to help out."

Even before I could ask why they made such a request, they told me, "I don't want Deacon X giving me communion."

I asked why one deacon would be different from another deacon in giving communion. They explained they had seen Deacon X doing things out in the community that just weren't "Christ-like." They continued by saying they don't watch me everywhere I go, but they know me and know my character, which went much further than I ever could think of. It's so important when it comes to the character, the respect, and the standards of a deacon, and that inspired me to write this book.

Many times we know how to perform our duties on Sunday, but when it comes to Monday through Saturday, we seem to have minimal impact in the community or among the members, because you never know who's watching you. When you get to the point where people begin to look to you for instruction, seek your guidance to procure resources, and see you as a leader in the church and the community, it shouldn't go to your head. It should drive you to do better to walk closer to Christ. Are we going to fall? Yes, because we all are going to make mistakes. Are we going to say things we shouldn't say? Yes, we are, but prayerfully, we have to know how to repent and say, "I apologize, forgive me," and ask the Lord for forgiveness.

CHAPTER 4

The Position

Thris chapter will give you a good foundational understanding of the actual position and qualifications for a deacon. We don't want you to walk away from this book not knowing the totality of this position and its expectations, as described in the Bible. It's one thing to have a purpose or calling for a position, but now, what are the position's qualifications? You may ask yourself the following questions:

"Can I meet those qualifications of a deacon?" At times, we may believe the new position we accepted, or the new job we are considering, may be a challenge for us, but with the proper training and support, we will be effective. "Will I be able to sustain those qualifications as a deacon effectively?" As I mentioned above, you need support from the pastor and other deacons in your walk as a deacon. Training doesn't stop once you are ordained as a deacon. Training is on a continual basis.

"How does my family look at this from the aspect of me having to fulfill these qualifications?" Your family knew you and your characteristics before you were a deacon, so they may be very honest in helping you in this new position, and it's important to share what you are going through while you are training so they understand your concerns.

"Are they supportive of me?" Gaining support from your spouse, family, the pastor, deacons, and church membership is important in your position as a deacon. As a leader, you want to have the pulse of the congregation to minimize any murmuring as well as know what the people need in resources and prayers.

When you go into any leadership position, it's not only you; your family also goes along with you in that position. With that in mind, our training covers this to make sure you understand what's expected of you in this position. As you will discover during the interview before you are nominated for ordination, this aspect of leadership will be an essential factor. These questions will be asked, and you will have to not only answer them, but show in your proven work that you can fulfill these different qualifications for the position of a deacon.

Now, does every deacon have every qualification of a deacon to the point where they're walking on air? No, but they should possess the selection requirements being of honest report, full of the Holy Ghost and wisdom. Are they so perfect they don't need any work to do on themselves? No, that is not true. I sat in on interviews with many deacons before their ordination, and we made recommendations that they should go back and do more work, or we need to take a closer look at them later on, or they need more work in certain areas.

The pastor and church should ask the ordination council to provide in detail what they observed to make their decision to not go forward. Just because we like people or they are nice doesn't mean they can fulfill the duty of a deacon. Factors that would delay or stop the process include a lack of honesty or wisdom, or displays of the Holy Spirit during questioning. At that point, it's up to the pastor and the church if they want to continue with the ordination date. It's a challenge when pastors schedule the ordination interview on a Saturday, and the next day is the ordination service. You may have family members coming from out of town and church members preparing for the service, so the interviewing council are pressed to pass this person and make the recommendation to move forward with the ordination, which is not pleasing to God and could negatively impact the church. My recommendation is to not set up the Sunday ordination service until the candidate passes the ordination council's interview.

Deacons will often be privy to information that can't be shared with the spouse, family members, or anyone outside the initial conversation. For example, there are times when you go to the hospital for a visit. When the doctor or nurse enters the patient's room, the first thing you should do is excuse yourself and step out of the room, whether you finished your visitation or not. This not only gives the patient privacy, but due to the HIPAA law, certain information can't be shared without the patient's consent. Churches are not held accountable by this law, because we are not a healthcare provider, but I ask the church to always follow the guidance of moral ethics and not to ask or share the patient's condition verbally (during announcements, meetings, prayer calls) or in bulletins or meeting minutes.

I don't advise going back to the church during Bible study or on Sunday morning, revealing, "We went to go see Brother Jonathan and his blood pressure was high, they had him on an intravenous medication, and his doctor said the liver they removed didn't have a trace of cancer."

The member may say, "It's okay, you can stay in the room with the nurse; they are just taking my vitals." Politely excuse yourself and let the patient know you will be right back. Don't stand near the patient's door; walk down the hall where you can observe the doctor or nurse leaving the member's room, so that you can return, but can't overhear any conversations. When you do come back, plan to end your visit soon. It's important when you arrive to be quiet during your visit. Don't talk, pray, or sing loudly in the patient's room, because it is a hospital, and you don't want to disturb others who are resting. Feel free to ask family, friends, or other patients in the room if they want to join you all in prayer.

If you bring communion for your member, stop by the nurse's station before entering the patient's room to get permission first, because the patient may be fasting or can't have the wafer or juice. You can even ask if the patient is feeling well enough for a visit, but nothing else about the patient. Be succinct in your conversation during the visit. Execute the plan you discussed earlier before the visit (e.g., greeting, scripture, prayer, song, and small talk). Doing this will ensure the visit was fulfilled if you had to step away. If by chance you do hear something about a patient's medical condition, notice the medication being given, or are told something by a healthcare professional, do not repeat that information. Each church should have moral ethical guidelines in place for all to follow.

There are moments when you are at church, and someone will pull you to the side and say, "Hey, I need assistance with rent. I need assistance with utilities due to my job cutting our hours [or a spouse is sick or left the home]. I need assistance with housing, because right now, my children and I are sleeping in the car."

That type of information should not be shared with anyone else other than those making the decision to help; the details can be discussed openly in the deacon's meeting or with mission leaders. The person's personal information is not to be shared with anyone in the church or your home. If you were to disclose this private information to your family, you have broken the ethical code of being a deacon and created a situation where your family begins to view the person differently. For example, they may begin to judge that person in a different way, not knowing the details of the conversation. When personal information comes to you, you need to be able to keep that within yourself. Your spouse has to understand that information should not be shared from any meeting you attend.

Important note: When people share they are having thoughts of suicide or hurting someone else (or themselves), or a child discloses abuse, refer them to the proper resources or law enforcement authorities. You may need to stay with the member until the authorities arrive or they have made contact with a resource agency. You will want to notify your spouse of what you are doing (if the member is a female, they can assist) without disclosing the person's personal information.

What Does a Deacon Look Like?

Deacon Qualifications

1 Timothy 3:8–10, 12–13 (KJV) says, "Likewise must the Deacons be grave, not double-tongued, not given to much wine, not greedy of filthy lucre; holding the mystery of faith in a pure conscience. And let these also first be proved; then let them use the office of a Deacon, being found blameless. Let the Deacons be the husband of one wife, ruling their children and their own houses well. For they that have used the office of a Deacon well purchase to themselves a good degree, and great boldness in the faith which is in Christ Jesus."

> **Must be grave:** The deacon must be honest.
>
> **Not double-tongued:** The deacon must not say different things to different people about the same subject.
>
> **Not given to much wine:** The deacon should not overindulge in wine.
>
> **Not greedy of filthy lucre:** The deacon should not pursue dishonest gain.

Holding the mystery of the faith in a pure conscience: The deacon must maintain a good conscience and power of faith.

First be proved: Deacons should not be a new convert. They must be tested, and if nothing is found against them, they can serve as a deacon.

Found blameless: The deacon must be free of evil reproach.

Husband of one wife: The deacon must not be a polygamist.

Ruling their children and their household well: Deacons should manage their children and household well before being considered to be a leader in the church.

As stated earlier, the formal selection of deacons by the church sometimes had a different search criteria than the text above. Deacons were at times selected based on the large amount of money they put in the offering plate each Sunday. The deacon's selection was sometimes based on if he had a business in the community or had a prominent position in the community, and some were selected due to their advanced age. In other words, this selection search was looking for an important or older person rather than the biblical qualifications. Can you imagine the impact on the church membership of selecting someone based on how much they financially funded the church? This means they can dictate the direction of the church based upon their giving or holding out their giving. When you select a deacon based upon a prominent person in the community, their relevance lasts as long as they are well-known in the community. When a deacon is selected based on owning a business, it can impact the ministry, because they most times work on a return on investment (ROI) rather than the Holy Spirit. If that owner is not someone with a business acumen, then you just selected a figurehead who will not be an asset to the ministry. However, utilizing the qualifications that God set forth, the deacon is prepared to not only care for the people, but to support the pastor. Having the qualifications listed above will not make you a perfect person for the position of a deacon, but they will be an asset to the ministry, pastor, and community.

We have to follow the scripture in Proverbs 3:5–6: "Trust in the Lord with all thine heart, and lean not unto thine own understanding. In all thy ways acknowledge Him, He shall direct thy path." We need God's direction to guide us when selecting leaders in the church: pastor, deacons, trustees, board chairs, teachers, all the way through to contractors that work in the building. Making the wrong selection for any leader can negatively shape the face of the church, which will not be productive and create a lot of church hurt.

Growing up under positive leadership has positioned me to be able to work with many church and community leaders as a church consultant. We often hear about bad leadership, but rarely lift up good leadership. For example, when eating at a restaurant, one would quickly call over the manager when you received bad service, but how many times have you called over the manager to say how well the server handled your table? Try it next time you receive good service or have a problem solved by a customer service person. You don't realize the impact you made on that person; it will encourage them to keep providing good service; God will recognize them even through others. Ask to speak to their manager to explain how well you enjoyed that person helping you.

Is this something we do in the church? Do we thank God for the good leadership we have, because I know we tell Him about the bad. Pray and ask God to send you more good leadership to help enhance and grow your ministry. Professor Sophia Matthews writes, "Deacons are leaders and should be held to Christian Biblical standards, not church standards." The Bible clearly details the responsibilities for Christian leaders in the New Testament messages to the different churches. I believe deacons are called to perform service and assist the pastor and the lay members. However, they are often appointed only to help a pastor achieve his personal agenda, and not God's vision. The number of deacons should be proportionate to church membership in order for them to be effective. For instance, a church with two thousand members should have enough deacons to serve a reasonable number of members without being overwhelmed and overworked. On the other hand, there should not be twenty deacons in a fifty-membership congregation.

Qualifications for Spouses

Now one might ask, are there "qualifications for the spouse of a deacon? The answer is yes. In 1 Timothy 3:11, the King James Version says, "Even so must their wives be grave, not slanderers, sober, faithful in all things." When considering the spouse, it's important to review the qualifications to prepare the spouse for the deacon's training, ordination, and service beyond. There are times when a deacon has accepted his position and dedicates his service to the Lord, but when it comes to the spouse, she may have a different perspective of her role; she may not realize she plays a major part, not only as a wife, but as a deaconess. Being a partner in a marriage, you may have to try new things or do something different for the betterment of the relationship. I remember my wife and I joined the krav maga training program (krav maga is a self-defense system developed by the Israel Defense Forces for training military personnel in hand-to-hand combat); we joined along with our grandson Cameron. This was another opportunity for me to spend time with my wife and exercise. During one Sunday 11:00 a.m. service, I used the training as a sermon illustration. I explained how, by accident, this very slender young lady walked into my punch. I pulled the punch with distance not to hit her, but her momentum carried her into my hand. As I was explaining the illustration, I mentioned how I didn't enjoy the class, but wanted to go to support my wife, which was my objective. When reviewing a leadership position you are considering, it is important to make sure your spouse understands every aspect of the role she plays in supporting you and your loved ones.

In some relationships, the spouse may support the deacon, but she has no desire to be a deaconess. This is an important conversation that must be done sooner rather than later during the training process. Can you imagine never having this conversation to understand the thoughts of the spouse in becoming a deaconess, and you just assume she is onboard with the training?

As a pastor, we would be creating a toxic home environment for that new deacon trying to force or blindly lead his wife into a position she had no desire to fulfill or may not be morally ready for, in her eyes. Our deacon certification training covers these aspects as well as helps the couple work through those issues. Through leadership training and awareness, more empathy should be given to the deaconess during the training.

Not all deaconesses are ready to put on the white uniform on the first Sunday and wear the same type of hat as those that've been a deaconess for decades. Be mindful of the style of clothes a senior deaconess would wear, compared to a younger woman. Be mindful of clothing costs and how every style doesn't look the same on every woman. I remember when the deacons wanted to buy suits all the same style and color. The store they went to you could get two suits, three dress shirts, two pairs of socks, and four ties for $99.99. Number one: You remember I told you that Deacon Waddell taught us how to dress at a young age, and that wasn't the type of store I would purchase clothes from. Number two: How long were these clothes going to last? Leadership should be mindful of how the current group of deaconesses Approach and treat the new deaconess regardless of age with fairness and love. Get to know the spouse of the deacon through fellowship and not interrogation methods. There's a big difference and spiritual impact between fellowship and interrogation. True fellowship is open and inviting, but interrogation tactics will lead to marital conflicts for the new deacon in training, because the spouse will express to her husband how she was mistreated and by whom. Remember, perception is 100 percent valid in the mind of the person experiencing the situation. Not only have those that mistreated her created church hurt, but they placed the deacon in training in a situation of whether he supports his wife or his calling. Due to the lack of training and empathy by the current deaconess, you may have not only lost a deaconess, but a church member too. It can take a long time to get over church hurt. If a deacon candidate wants to continue his training, but his wife doesn't want to be a part of the ministry as a deaconess, it's important to have the conversation as soon as possible with the pastor and chairman of the Deacon Board.

Support of the Children

The support of the children of a deacon, regardless of age, is important. This is a conversation that should happen within the family setting. You should take time to explain to your children about the position you have been selected for. The older the children, the more detail can be shared. Make sure this is an exciting conversation highlighting that you were selected as a deacon by God and His people. Explain to the children about your purpose in serving the church and inform them about the qualifications you and your spouse have to follow for these positions. When you are a leader, whether in the church or the community, your children become a part of your leadership, and they may hear things or see things you don't hear or see what others are saying about you. Your children may be the targets of other people trying to get back at you or trying to get your attention.

After my daughters became older, they shared with me that certain women in the church were attracted to me, and they knew this due to the church rumor mill (they never shared their names, but they still joke about it today from time to time). Even though I didn't notice any advances, they explained what they saw and how someone looked at me. They also said, "We hear what she says about you, which leads us to believe that she likes you." Alternatively, there's always the flip side of hearing how people dislike you, and it makes them upset, because now they show negative feelings towards those people. That's something you have to deal with in the home, which you will have to talk about and discuss. Yes, you may laugh it off, but you have to wonder if this is an issue you need to be aware of, because you may need to put out the smoke before it becomes a fire.

When your children play with other children, they may see things or talk about things, or when they go over to their friend's house, they may talk about things occurring in your home. If you don't have respect in your house, then there may be an opportunity where a child may tell a friend or the friend's parents. My uncle, the late Pastor Johnny W. Brewster, often said from the pulpit on Sunday morning, "I know when you talk about me in your home, because the children don't speak to me on Sundays." Well, this is what happens when we take information from the church and talk about it in the car in front of the kids. Regardless of age, in the car, or in the home, you should not have adult conversations in front of the children. They get a different perspective of that person you're talking about, and they may act differently towards that person the next time they see them.

It is a practice of mine, and I will share it with you: "Don't have adult conversations around children." I often encounter adults doing this, but I will say, "Let's talk later." I stop talking, because they missed the point, and soon after, I excuse myself or end the call. Supporting your children as a deacon should not change from before you were selected to be a deacon. Attending their school activities and sporting events, keeping in touch with what's important to your children, especially preteens, and making sure family outings are not overlooked. It may become challenging to attend meetings, visit and call members, and support your pastor in the midst of performing your duties if you don't have a balanced home and ministry life.

Support of Your Extended Family

However, your extended family, which may be your siblings, parents, in-laws, or cousins, knows you have a leadership position in the church, especially if it's a family church, and they all attend church together with you. When they ask you about different aspects of your job or what's going on within the church, you have to be prepared to address this in a loving manner, especially if there is some murmuring going on in the church and the deacons have already prayed for guidance and determined a plan of action based on the direction of the Holy Spirit. Those extended family members and friends may want to know more information. They may have seen Brother and Sister Doe come and talk to you, and just by chance ask you what they wanted to talk about. They may see a single mother come up to you and talk at length, then you are asked by your extended family, "Is it something we can do to help with Sister Doe? I seen her talking with you. Do they need help again?"

Due to your position in the church and following the moral, and ethical guidelines, you can't tell anyone's business, even to extended family and friends. The sooner everyone understands this aspect of your leadership position, the better you can fulfill your role. When this situation arises, it's okay to let everyone know you cannot share any information with them. If there happens to be murmuring around the church, feel free to let them know you are aware of the situation and the board is praying for direction from the Holy Spirit.

CHAPTER 5

The Parish

This chapter is about how deacons interact with the church. It is important that we understand how the deacon can be effective within the church as a leader. Oftentimes, the deacon is looked upon as a leader of the church, viewed as the go-to person in the church, and seen as a person of resource in the church. With all those different attributes, you have to make sure you are staying within the understanding of your purpose of honest rapport, full of the Holy Ghost and wisdom. This is why training is so important for any leader, especially in the church when you're dealing with the spiritual aspect of people's lives. We sometimes see people at their worst, and we see people at their best, and during both times, we must have the integrity and the trust of the membership, as well as those who walk through the doors of the church. Deacons should understand they are ordained to serve in their church only. If you go to another church, and they recognize you as a deacon and ask you to assist with the worship service, feel free to come up front or sit with the other deacons. But you may not be recognized as a deacon, so don't go straight up to the front pew without an invitation by the deacon of that church. If you're asked to pray, don't sing and pray. If you're asked to read a scripture, don't give a sermonette before or after. Just do what they ask you to do.

How Does a Deacon Perform His Basic Duties?

Performing the Ministry

While executing the ministry of a deacon, we will touch briefly on some areas, but spend time in detail in other aspects of the ministry. We review all areas in detail during our Acts 6 deacon certification training to prepare you for ordination. During the training, we will take time to go over the various aspects of the deacon's ministry, such as handling conflict in the church, facilitating a meeting, as well as locating and connecting with resources in your community. We also discuss the transition from the back pew to the front pew in leadership. This is where people used to sit next to you in the third or fourth pew every Sunday morning, but now you sit in the left front pew, your spouse sits in the right front pew, and now the family that used to sit together in the same spot now sits apart, which becomes a different family dynamic.

When I was called to the ministry, my pastor, Reverend S. John Barley, told me there would be a transition from being a deacon to a minister of the Gospel. As a deacon, I never thought about the transition from being a deacon to an associate minister, but he was right. Those deacons were the people I spent time with in meetings and services, spent time over their houses, and attended outings together. Now, because I'm a minister, I have to ask myself, "How will my transition in leadership change my relationship with my friends?" The relationship didn't change for the bad; it changed for the good, because there was an additional level of expectation and respect, and I will always appreciate them for that homage to my wife and I.

I will never forget one time when I sat at the pastor's table during an afternoon program. You know, the table that was set up different from the others. The table had a real tablecloth, not paper. The table with real silverware and china, not plasticware. During that dinner, I was back-to-back with the deacon's table in the middle of the fellowship hall.

Someone tapped me on the shoulder and asked, "Can you cut me a piece of that German chocolate cake?"

I said, "Sure."

Now, the pastor's table not only looked different, but it had a different selection of food. I quite naturally didn't know the protocol of sitting at the pastor's table in the South, because up

North in New Jersey, where I was from, my uncle had us all eat together. I cut the deacon a slice of cake and passed it over to him.

Then he whispered, "Can you cut me a piece of that other cake?"

I cut a piece of that other cake and passed it back to him. In my mind, these guys were my friends for the past couple of years, but now I'm at the pastor's table.

Reverend Barley whispered, "Look, if you want to continue to sit at this table, stop passing food back to the other tables. This is for us at this table."

The next request was quickly denied by me with a smile, because I liked being at the pastor's table. We laughed about it, but guess what, I didn't pass any more cake, because sitting at this table, the food was really good. Not that the other food wasn't good, but it just looked better on china plates. As a leader, you need to recognize that there will be higher levels of opportunity you will be invited to, that we will need to make adjustments in our decorum.

Providing Communication

When providing information within the church, it's best to find out the most effective way based on your relationship with the pastor, deacons, leaders, and other members. Now that we're into social media with new applications and smartphones, there are so many ways that information is passed along. When it comes to communicating within a relationship, do you need to know how the other person best receives communication, as well as your best areas of providing communication? Yes, just ask your spouse if you are a good communicator. Look at your job evaluations in the area of communication, which is a good indicator of how well you are doing. You might find out you do a lot of "drizzling" like my mother-in-law, the late Elizabeth Harris-Manson, would say if she heard you rambling on. When you speak, it's hard for people to follow you when you ramble. You may find during your conversation it's difficult for you to stay on subject, and you're all over the place with no end in sight. You may find it hard to focus when others are talking, and you keep interrupting them. You may learn that rabbit trails have been your friend for years when trying to explain something. Have you had a person cut you off from making a point, because they didn't want to forget their point?

Why is communication important to a deacon? Communicating with your pastor is important for your relationship as a leader in the church. How can you both work together efficiently, if you don't understand each other's way of communicating? If your pastor is the type of person who texts a lot and you're not, then at some point, you have to come up with a way to communicate with each other. If you like to be on the phone and have older people in the church who like to talk on the phone, then that works, but if you're a younger deacon, that may be a challenge for you.

The important part of communicating is to make sure everybody is aware of what information needs to be passed along, as well as the method. The same basic communication should be shared. Can you imagine different scenarios of a type of meeting getting out to the membership? One saying the pastor called a meeting; another saying the deacons called the pastor to a meeting. Another version is, the deacons called a church meeting. These various messages going out about a meeting can be devastating to a church due to the perception of the meeting version the person received. I worked nights over the years at my full-time jobs, and after I got off the night shift, I would stop by the church to handle some church business, attend Community meetings, attend church meetings, attend one-on-one meetings at the church, all before I went home to go to sleep. Be mindful. You still have to communicate with your spouse who was at work and children in school to make sure everybody knows what's going on or expected at home. Communication is paramount.

Passing out Communion

As we discussed, communion is one of the ordinances in the church, the other being baptism. The deacon and deaconess will get together to set up the trays of juice and wafers. For some time now, you can purchase juice in a cup, along with a wafer, packaged all together in one unit. However, be observant: Some people may have trouble opening the package and need assistance. The act of breaking the bread represents Christ's body being broken for us. Along with drinking the juice representing Christ's blood, which was shed for us, it should be explained to those taking part in that service that the wafer and juice are symbolic of the body and blood of Christ. You might offer a prayer of forgiveness or a period of time allowing others to silently ask God for forgiveness, so they don't bring damnation unto themselves, not discerning the Lord's body before taking communion. Some churches only serve it once a month, but other churches serve it every Sunday. It doesn't matter. In 1 Corinthians 11:26 (KJV), it says, "For as often as ye eat this bread, and drink this cup, ye do shew the Lord's death till he come."

There should be a systematic way of serving communion to the membership. If it's a small church, the ushers may ask that everyone move forward just before communion is served so the elements can be passed out in a timely manner. If it's a larger church, then there's a conventional process in serving the elements. Make sure that whatever process you use, the attention is not on the deacons marching around the church, but remembering Jesus Christ.

I've seen where the deacons would perform a choreographed marching band-style routine, passing out and collecting the elements. People should not come to video the deacon's march on communion Sunday, ending with a standing ovation. Who gets the glory of fulfilling that ordinance of the church? The dress is mostly a black suit and white shirt for men and a white dress for women, with both wearing white gloves. It's up to your church what dress code you select, but remember, if you select any other color than black, it may be challenging to obtain that color depending on the season, availability in stores in your area, as well as the sizes of that person. This is something we can review if needed during our Acts 6 certification training and suggest a process for your church with your pastor's approval.

Productive Visitation

There are times when you are asked to perform a home visitation for members who are sick or can't get out to the church due to mobility concerns or other reasons. Your church should establish procedures to follow for home visitation. Make sure you call ahead to find out a good day and time to do your home visitation. Remember, you can serve communion any day. When you do your home visitation, make sure you take someone with you, preferably your spouse, but if not, take another deacon with you or invite the pastor to come to share in that visitation. One time, I was over at my mother-in-law's house, the late Elizabeth Harris-Mason, and her pastor came by for visitation. It was a hot day in the summer, and he came in with regular clothes, jeans, and a shirt. You have to remember that with older people, they look up to those of us who have positions in the church, especially the pastor and deacon, which are the two ordained offices in the church. What they remember seeing you wear on Sunday at church is what they expect you to look like when you visit, especially when they fixed themselves up or had someone help dress them for your visit. The pastor might have been out and just stopped by that day with regular clothes on, if that was the case I would have called first to explain you were out and was thinking about them and wanted to stop by for a moment.

They talked for a short while, and then before he left, she told him, "The next time you come to visit me, make sure that you're dressed as a pastor should dress."

He acknowledged her words and departed.

I grew up with my grandmother, the late Louise Collins, and many times I've witnessed when the church came by to bring her communion or just visit. One of the deacons of the church would come with Mother Sarah Davis, who would always tell me as a young child that I would be a preacher. Unfortunately, she didn't live long enough to see the prophecy fulfilled. The deacon would come dressed in his black suit and white shirt, and Mother Davis would come in her white dress and a white hat. That was the kind of standard dress for a deacon and deaconess. Nowadays, you have to know your audience; if you're going to see a person in their home, dress according to how they see you on Sunday during service. If you dress down at church, and that's how they see you dressed all the time, then you can dress down when you go visit them. If they see you in a suit at church, they're naturally going to want to see you in a suit when you go visit them at home, in the hospital or a healthcare facility. I encourage you to dress at least business casual, because you represent your church leadership. You never know who you might meet during your visitation, which would impact their perception of the church leadership.

Make sure to develop a plan for your visit, before you walk into the person's home or facility. What I mean is, if you are going with the pastor, discuss who's going to lead the prayer, who's going to get the communion ready and serve it, who's going to sing a song, who's going to discuss the latest updates at the church (or whatever information you are going to share with that person). Have that all planned out so you look like you know what you're doing, and you're not bumbling and fumbling when you get there. For a new deacon, practice before you go. Sit down at the church or go out for coffee or lunch as a team before you visit the church member's home. Rehearse the same scenario you are going to perform during the visitation.

Sometimes, when you go to a person's home, they'll invite you over for lunch. Some of the older people do that, but if they invite you for lunch, feel free to join them, if you have a relationship with that person. Most times, you can politely decline. The visitation shouldn't be longer than thirty minutes, especially in a hospital or facility.

Protecting the Confidentiality of the Pastor and Members

We talked about confidentiality earlier in chapter 4, but I can't stress this enough; when it comes to confidentiality, deacons must follow the moral, ethical guidelines established by the church with the utmost of integrity. When you're a leader, and you're discussing a member's personal health, as well as information shared with you or discussed in front of you, make sure you keep that information to yourself. What you observed, heard, or were told should not be discussed with your spouse, in front of your children, or with anyone who wasn't in that room or in that situation. When people go to sign up for assistance, those who hand out food, provide resources, or write the check don't know all the details of the person requesting help. It's just on a need-to-know basis. This is something we take more time to review in greater detail during your Acts 6 deacon certification training.

Did the church member explain to you they're going to the hospital for surgery? It's not a good idea, morally or ethically, to ask what type of surgery they're having. Helpful tips for this and other similar situations are, don't ask if they found cancer; that's the person's private information, and it is not to be shared. I know sometimes, when we want to pray, we want to pray and ask God for specific things. You can still pray and ask God to cover that person, even though you don't know the specifics of it, but God does.

I went to Uganda on two occasions, preaching a revival and teaching with Pastor Andre McGuire, who invited me to accompany him both times. We would preach at night and teach Bible study during the day. After I taught Bible study one afternoon, a very young girl came up to me and pulled on my jacket to get my attention. While she was pulling on my jacket, other people came up to me, greeting me. You know how they greet you and shake your hand after you preach a sermon at church. It got to the point where she kept tugging. Finally, I looked down and greeted her, and she started talking in her native tongue, but I didn't understand what she was saying. I asked the interpreter to translate what she was saying.

Her message was, "My aunt is sick. Can you come pray for her?"

I asked the interpreter where her aunt was, so we could pray for her. I thought the aunt was with her at Bible study. The little girl told the interpreter where the aunt lived. It was what they called the "bush country," which was far from the city in Uganda where we were. I then asked him to interpret what I was saying and explain to the young girl that we could pray for her aunt right there, right now, and if it is God's will, He will bless and heal her, and that's just what we did. I didn't ask the young girl what was wrong with her aunt. I didn't ask her to add details. God knows the details. All we have to do is pray to Him on her behalf. Having this understanding and knowledge base keeps us out of legal problems, keeps people in the congregation from knowing someone else's personal business, continues to build trust for you as a leader, and ultimately allows God's will to manifest.

CHAPTER 6

The Power

his chapter discusses the power of the deacon, because with every leadership position, there's always someone in power. When you're a leader and have some authority where people report to you, there's always the possibility of not being effective in your position. Consequently, abuse of power may become evident in a leadership position. Because of this, I feel it is critical to address in this book, specifically when highlighting the importance of the deacon. I've been fortunate enough to work with different types of leaders with significant positions in the community and corporations. I've found that their integrity and honesty are always at the forefront when it comes to the people of the community.

One night, while we were at a community event, I was asked to be on the executive board of the Gwinnett County NAACP by Mrs. Pat, the chapter president at that time. After I explained my hesitancy, she explained in detail what she was trying to do. After a lengthy conversation, the last thing she said to me that made me join her was, "Reverend, if you're looking to make political gain in Gwinnett County, don't join, because I have enough of them." Her last statement made me feel that Mrs. Pat was about business in helping the people and not status. She and I worked together for a couple of years until she moved out of the county. I left soon after the next president came, because he was about status, with no accomplishments.

How many know that once you become a leader, your personal life becomes a public life, even in the church? In the eyes of church members, leaders, such as the pastor and deacon, are very significant. If you make one mistake, the congregation will hold you accountable for your actions. Remember in chapter 3, I discussed how a member didn't want their deacon to serve them communion, because of what they saw him doing? In other words, your leadership has been discounted to the point where neither church members nor community members wish to work with you any longer.

I knew deacons in the past who publicly argued and fought with pastors, and negativity brought down the office of a deacon through their own actions which were contrary to the qualifications found in Acts 6 and 1 Timothy 3, simply because they disagreed with the pastor or did not like what he said or did. In the Acts 6 deacon certification training, we teach conflict resolution to enable deacons to resolve issues and concerns before it comes to a shouting match.

Is There Power in the Office of a Deacon?

The Face: Myth or Reality

Therefore, when it comes to the myth or reality of the office of a deacon, it's important that we overlay the myth with reality. Many times, people have an idea of how a deacon should look, based on their perception and the performance of other deacons. This furthers the myth of how a deacon should act, dress, walk, and talk, which can be contrary to the scripture for the office of a deacon. There's always been a myth that the deacon who can sing the best already had a couple of drinks before church. The deacon who prays the longest often repeats the same prayer each time, because you can recite the prayer with him. So often, we think the deacon should always wear a black suit on the first Sunday. On the second Sunday, they wear a light color suit; on the third Sunday, the deacon might wear a brown suit, and on the fourth Sunday, a gray suit. This dress code was to ensure everyone was in uniform. But as time goes on and the world changes, the myth is that the deacon should change with the world. There should be a new style, a new look, a new walk, a new talk based on the world's current standards. However, the reality is that Acts chapter 6 describes the purpose of the deacon, and in 1 Timothy 3, the qualifications of a deacon are explained. Therefore, that's the standard.

The reality is that churches have changed. No longer are they wearing suits every Sunday, nor are they sitting in pews every Sunday or singing with pianos, nor are parishioners physically at church, as a result of our digital world. Due to COVID-19, many churches have successfully done live streaming and continue on, so at what point in time do we evolve the position of the deacon? As part of the Acts 6 deacon certification training, we understand during our discussions, we may not come to a definitive solution, but should be aware that change will take place in the life of the church. For example, not all churches look the same. There are different cultures in the church currently, with different family makeups. Therefore, we have to adapt and understand those different dynamics. As a church body, do we change to the world's standards or keep in alignment with the Bible? Although we live in a changing world, that doesn't give us the right to judge others, because we all will have to answer to God one day.

The Faith (Internal Leader)

When considering the other attributes of the deacon, what is equally important is faith. The ordination committee observes the external characteristics of the leader to see how well they handle themselves in their position, how well they personally balance family, ministry, and work life, how well they are adapting to the position, and how the membership is adapting to them. Those aspects of the position of a deacon can shake your faith if you don't manage them. To take this a step further, it's important that we sit down and discuss some of the dynamics of what a deacon goes through. We review this in Acts 6 deacon certification training sessions, understanding the concepts of internally looking at oneself periodically for a balanced life.

Additionally, it is strongly recommended that you regularly check in with an accountability partner, a mentor, or somebody who makes sure you are stable and fit for duty as a leader. Most times, pastors don't always have a safe environment to speak what's on their heart without being criticized, and that's where a deacon can provide a listening ear for the pastor. As a deacon, you should always have someone you can discuss your concerns with.

At JL Watts Enterprise, LLC, we provide that safe place. Our team has created a space where deacons fellowship online to discuss their issues and receive encouragement from other deacons. This time of sharing each month through our mentorship is vitally important, because it allows deacons to speak freely and get responses from people who are in that position as well. Just imagine having a deacon like Leonard Blackshear to sit down and talk to, with his calming voice encouraging you and giving you feedback.

Throughout my lifetime, many professional women have inspired me. I could talk to them to make sure my internals were balanced. I could share information, knowing it wouldn't go anywhere else, but stay right there. As leaders, we should always look for people who will encourage us in a way that helps us and doesn't hurt us. For example, I had Mother Alberta Dawkins, who always made sure you were comfortable coming over to her house, whether we were eating her food or she brought food to the church. She was very serious as well. She wanted you to eat that food and make sure you were comfortable while eating and talking, as she would ask you questions about what was going on in your life.

Another example of being encouraged was when I could call on Mom and Pop, James and Beulah Smith. Those two people lived down the street from me for many years before they retired and moved to North Carolina. Our conversations were always encouraging. They took time to talk with me, looked me up and down, because they wanted to know how I was doing. They would ask, "How's your family doing? What have you been doing lately?" When I looked into their eyes and saw the sincerity of them speaking to me, it was an uplifting experience.

As a pastor or deacon, do you have anyone you can call on to be your mentor? If you do not, reach out to us, and one of our trainers will be available to help guide you through these difficult times; they can be mentors to you throughout the certification program.

The Fun (External Leader)

Every leader should be able to take time out of their busy schedule and create an opportunity for fun. You should have a hobby doing something you enjoy outside of ministry. My wife is always telling me I need a hobby. If you're a leader and don't take time out for fun for yourself, your spouse, or your family, you won't be a well-rounded leader. People want to see you smile, to see you live, and to see you in different aspects of life. Just imagine the deacons taking the pastor out to a professional sports game. What about the deacons taking the pastor out to a show with all the spouses? Can you imagine the bonding between the pastor and the deacons? What about an outing for the deacons and their families? What about a church outing, including the children, ensuring they also have fun? What about a local activity that involves you giving back to the community, as well as having fun?

These are all aspects of having a balanced life within the church as a leader, especially a deacon.

There will be times and opportunities during those different activities that someone may share something with you that you didn't previously know about, or you get to learn something about them. It all turns into a fun experience, creating a closer relationship.

CHAPTER 7

The Pastor

Too often, we overlook the relationship between the deacon and the pastor. That relationship is very vital to the health and the welfare of the church. When there is division between the pastor and deacons, then there is division within the church body, and everyone knows about it and is very apparent every Sunday morning. To overcome all that, it's important to understand the role of a deacon. When you walk in that role and fulfill it as an effective leader, you can have the strength to understand the relationship that will be seen throughout the congregation, and God will be pleased. Unfortunately, I've witnessed many occurrences where deacons and pastors have butted heads. I had a deacon approach me in a parking lot while on my way to my car, and I told him, "Before I go to sleep tonight, I will give God your name." He just stood there, so I got in my car and left.

Some members in the congregation don't understand what it takes to be a pastor, the sacrifice, dedication, and commitment. It's hard to work with different personalities that want your attention as well as try to influence you for their gain. Having a healthy and strong relationship with the pastor also helps keep tabs on the pastor's integrity. There may be a time when the pastor almost crosses the line in certain areas, and you're able to encourage them from falling and encourage them not to go that route, because of the relationship you have. I talked about this earlier in chapter 1; my uncle and I used to go to the side room and have conversations about certain things before we brought them out to the congregation. Why do we do this? One-on-one between a pastor and deacon, two touching and agreeing for direction and clarity from God, is a sign of unity. When you come out of the back room, you are on one accord, saying publicly the same thing you said in private. How many times have we seen our government leaders say something in private that gets out into the public, and because it's out, everyone is now aware of it and hears it, and it's the saddest thing on that government leader's character?

How Does the Relationship between Pastor and Deacon Become One?

Relationship with the Pastor (Empathy)

The relationship between the deacon and the pastor can be amazing. It can be such a relationship that one knows the other so well that when working together, you already know different aspects of the pastor, what they look for, and what they need. I'm not talking about what they want in their coffee, the type of gas they use in their car, or which cleaners they take their dress clothes to. I'm referring to knowing when they are worried, disturbed, tired, stressed, excited, focused, and have spent time with the Lord by their message on Sunday or preaching a Saturday Night Special.

Understand that there will be people who interject their personal thoughts, but under the cover of the pastor. I will never forget when I was in a meeting with the trustees, and one of the leaders discussing changes to the church building kept saying, "The pastor doesn't want that," or "He wouldn't want this."

Remembering our previous conversations, we never discussed that, and we talked every single morning. He would call me, and we would discuss various things at the church. Some of the things this person said were not things I knew him to say. There comes a time when you know the pastor or other leaders so well that you know what their wish is. They felt their position authorized them to talk on behalf of the pastor rather than allowing the trustees to obtain clarification from the pastor directly. There is a quote by Pastor Shantell D. Hopkins, who said, "Pastors serve by leading and Deacons lead by serving." The pastor is the one who makes sure God's vision is fulfilled. The deacon can be the one who helps fulfill that vision God gave the pastor by spending time understanding the pastor's vision well enough to articulate it to the congregation.

The relationship between the pastor and deacon should not be a volatile one. If you're a leader, and it ever gets to the point where you're in a volatile situation with a coworker or your manager, this should be a time to recognize the need to check your internals. You need to take a step back and pray to the Holy Spirit for understanding, guidance, as well as direction; it is not the purpose of a deacon to run the pastor and tell the pastor what to do. That's why this book is so important to highlight and discuss the actual purpose and qualifications of a deacon, so you can be effective in the local church. Being an effective leader is something good leaders attain each and every day.

Relationship with the Pastor's Family

Having a positive relationship with the pastor's family is important. Being an effective deacon means encouraging the pastor's family in times of need. A leader is someone you can go to for resources, understanding, empathy, help, and encouragement. Just imagine your spouse talking to the pastor's spouse, confidentially, to be a sounding board or an empathetic ear, to get some heartfelt encouragement or just empathy when people are talking about the pastor and creating issues and problems in their relationship.

The pastor's spouse also needs someone to talk to; what if your spouse could be that person? How effective can you be as a leader in the body of Christ at the local church? There have been times I've been called out to different family dynamics, being a police chaplain, a deacon, and a pastor. It was part of my duty, and I was glad they did reach out. I was glad I had the skills and personality they needed, so I could share some words of comfort and empathy toward the families. These are the kind of people you meet and are hopefully able to connect with. Our Acts 6 deacon certification training program has a monthly meeting of deacons (at times, ministers and pastors join in). We meet on a monthly basis and discuss different aspects of the church, leadership, and the community. If that's something you don't have now, feel free to reach out and become a part of that monthly mentorship. You will be encouraged to learn how to be an effective leader in this program.

Working with the Pastor

As I stated before in chapter 6, when working with the pastor, you begin to create a bond or relationship that goes far beyond the office. Working with the pastor means attending different community meetings, as well as meetings with other pastors in other churches. If you're that type of deacon who will go with the pastor to meetings and know how to conduct yourself so you're looked upon as a leader, as an advocate for Christ, the pastor, and the church, but even a community leader, then you will gain so many resources meeting different people in your community, compared to those deacons who find it a waste of their time to get involved within their community.

When I was a deacon, the pastor took me to many community meetings and meetings with other pastors. I often offered to pick up the pastors and drive him. I remember driving Pastor S. John Bartley and Rev. Dondi Jones to the Stephen Olford Institute to study exegetical preaching. Sister Dorothy Bartley made us some of her famous fried chicken for the trip. Bartley and Jones were telling jokes the entire time. Bartley told a joke about his medicine that almost had me pull over to regain my composure. I had the opportunity more than the other leaders because I worked the third shift, allowing me to be more flexible during the day with my schedule, and I was available most days. Not only did we meet, but we would have lunch after some meetings and discuss if the information from the meeting could be implemented into the ministry.

Rev. Dr. Karen Black always gave me opportunities, even as a preacher, to assist her in her church preaching, sitting on ordination councils for other preachers as well as teaching, so it doesn't stop at being a deacon. Oftentimes, the pastor will be so elated that someone was able to go with them to various events to not only bring back information to the church first-hand, but just for the fellowship, being able to share and discuss different things during that time together, working for the church and the Lord. Working in the church, sometimes the pastor is down to doing some things, and if you're available to go down there during the hours that they're there, you can discuss different matters of the church. When people come by, and the pastor is by himself, having another person come and sit in the room when you talk with someone is such a big help, not having to take on member concerns by yourself. Sometimes, when an angry church member or parishioner wants to speak to the pastor, simply having that deacon there during that meeting is a great help. The pastor can minister while you just meditate, pray, and observe during the meeting. If you want to be that type of deacon, if you want to be that type of leader, then obtain the necessary training to be an effective Acts 6 deacon.

Pastor George W. Windley Jr. wrote the following:

> I have been blessed to have great and supportive
> deacons in my twelve years as pastor of the First

Baptist Missionary Church in Sumter, SC. In these twelve years, we have had the same Chair of Deacons, and our relationship is a great one. And it was not until speaking with some of my colleagues that I realized that what my Chair and I have is not what other pastors have with their deacons.

With that, I would say that the relationship between the deacon and the pastor can be an amazing relationship when both learn to be friends with one another. This is a growing process, as it takes time to learn one another. But in that time, the two parties will discover each other's personalities, their hearts, strengths, and weaknesses. The two will learn how to have each other's back and support the other. The two can have relationships outside the church and have fun with each other away from the sanctuary (for example, attending football games together, fishing, going out to eat, etc.). In fact, I was with my Chair when I met my wife. He was there with me when I was introduced to her. And so, after I proposed to my wife, he was one of the first I called, as he was there the day I met her.

The pastor/deacon relationship can be amazing when both parties respect each other. Deacons should see the pastor as a servant of God whose task is to teach and preach God's Word, equip and empower the saints, and spread the Word through missions. The deacon should not feel the pastor is in it for himself and therefore should not feel threatened or seek power away from the pastor. Deacons should respect the leadership placed on the pastor and share in the responsibilities in leading and serving the people.

In like manner, the pastor should respect the role of the deacon and see them as helpers, assistants in ministering to the people and spreading the Word of God. The common goal should be to worship God, serve God, and serve the people. Despite what pedestals the people place us on, we, the pastor and deacon, are mere servants, and with that, we are to respect each other in order to help each other, as we serve both the people and God.

The pastor/deacon relationship is like a team. If you were to watch football, basketball, or any other team sport, no matter what an individual player may accomplish on the court or field, their teammates are there to congratulate them, cheer with them, celebrate as that home run, 3-pointer, or touchdown helps the team win. So it is in God's Kingdom. We are one team. The pastor and deacon should operate as teammates; one prays, the other preaches, one visits this family, the other attends a youth event, and so on. Celebrate victories together, have huddles before service, encourage the pastor after his sermon, tell the deacon how well he sang that song, and so on. And sometimes, teammates may not always get along or see the same thing. Sometimes, the team may take an "L." But if we are filled with the Holy Spirit, we will be empowered to endure any hardships and any difficulties.

And lastly, the pastor/deacon relationship will be an amazing relationship when we put God first in all we do. From our preaching, our teaching, every meeting we attend and preside over, God must be first. As stated earlier, we are both mere servants, called and appointed to serve God and His people. As one of my members likes to say, "It's not about us, but all about Jesus." When the pastor or the deacon try to push their agendas and not God's, it opens the door for trouble. When the pastor or the deacon promote themselves and their opinions, their titles, their power, and not promote Christ and His ways, the relationship is in trouble.

The pastor/deacon relationship should mimic the relationship Jesus had with His disciples. They ate together, walked together, and ministered together. When Jesus told the disciples to go out, they did. When He performed the miracle of feeding the multitude, it was the disciples who sat everyone down, passed out the food, and picked up the leftovers. They worked as a team, with Christ as the leader. But it was the leader who washed their feet as He taught them about being humble and being a servant. And when Jesus ascended back into heaven, it was His disciples who were there, gathered together, watching Him go up. They were together up to the end. This is how the pastor and deacon relationship can be an amazing one: being together.

Searching for a Pastor

When it comes to searching for a pastor whose office is vacant, the next ordained official in most Baptist churches is the deacon. At that point, there's a call for a Pulpit Search Committee to be formed. That Pulpit Search Committee should have the guidance of the Holy Spirit and understanding of the congregation on what type of pastor the church body is looking for, through the guidance of the Holy Spirit. This is not the time for the deacons to take charge, take over, and lord it over the congregation, just because there's no pastor in place. This is the time to maintain the membership and make sure God's Word is being taught and preached with integrity by making sure leaders are in place, such as Bible study teachers and guest preachers, until a new pastor is selected. There are times when the deacon has to make sure there's someone in the pulpit every Sunday to preach God's Word until they have a pastor. Again, this is not the time to have a take-charge attitude. This is a time for teamwork, much prayer, strategic planning, and preparation, and a time to put together a search committee that is open and willing to hear from the Lord.

I have been a member and candidate of many search committees, as well as consulting with them, and it can be an emotional and spiritual strain on the life of the church. This is why it's important to have planning in place. I've seen capable associate ministers overlooked to maintain the continuity of the church, instead of considering them as a pastor. Some churches have been looking for a pastor for two to five years, and they're still calling different preachers to come every Sunday and preach there, with no end in sight. The church isn't growing, and there's no leadership in place. A church mentor or coach can consult with the committee, provide leadership training, and suggest interim pastors. At JL Watts Enterprise, LLC, we can assist your search committee.

I've been a candidate and met with the deacon, and they call you to come to preach and teach, and ask you to send your resume. They have you fill out an application, then ask you to respond to hundreds of questions that I'm quite sure nobody's reading. They may send your spouse fifty questions to answer too. Can you imagine being on the Deacon Board and the last training you attended was before your ordination, and this is the first time you're leading a pastoral search committee, with no insight or mutual outside guidance? Wouldn't you like to have someone to call to ask questions, someone with your best interest at heart, because you've already established a relationship during monthly meetings? Proverbs 29:18 says, "Where there is no vision, the people perish." How long can a church go on without a pastor and a vision in place? At times, you ask another local pastor, and they end up getting the church to hire them or someone close to them, which may not be who the church needs or God wants. That's why having a mentor or coach who is objective can be a great asset to you as a deacon.

CHAPTER 8

Conclusion

The seven steps to becoming an Acts 6 deacon are outlined in each chapter of this book: The Pacesetter, The Profile, The Purpose, The Position, The Parish, The Power, and The Pastor. Completing these seven steps in the Deacons Certification Training will prepare you for your deacon's ordination.

As I summarize the seven steps to becoming an Acts 6 deacon below, understand that your training does not end after your church ordination. Continual education for a deacon will ensure that you stay relevant, but the additional training is an asset to the pastor and the local church.

In chapter 1, we discussed the importance of understanding the standards for a deacon set by those deacons who came before us years ago. Those deacons I mentioned set the foundational standards for me, and I understood the need to further my education, as well as teach others. As a deacon, you should be encouraged to utilize your spiritual gifts and talents in your position within your church, as God has blessed you. Likewise, is there a deacon you know who inspired you to become who you are today, someone you strive to be like?

Chapter 2 highlighted the importance of knowing what the deacon looks like in different aspects of their life. In the home, the church, the workplace, and the community, deacons are observed most of all in their ministry. I imagine these are the areas where the church observed the person before they became a deacon. During the deacon's certification training, we help identify the areas of weakness for a deacon candidate, as well as build upon the strengths. Approaching training from this aspect helps increase your home life, church duties, workplace, and community balance to minimize stress and burnout.

As stated in chapter 3, the purpose of a deacon is often overlooked, but Acts 6:1–8 references the selection of a deacon.

Many times, we look at 1 Timothy 3:8–9, referencing the five characteristics as the only qualifications for a deacon. We should not disregard those qualifications, but we should make sure we understand the selection process of the office first. If you are not of honest rapport and full of the Holy Ghost and wisdom, then you were not even considered. Once the purpose of any position is understood and developed, the more effective you become, and the results are overwhelmingly high. Deacons who fully understand their position can care for their members. As explained in the book, the training will teach you the totality of what this position is, as described in the Bible.

Chapter 4 explained that when you go into any leadership position, remember, it's not only about you. Your family also goes along with you. We discussed how deacons will be privy to information that cannot be shared with their spouse, family members, or anyone outside the initial conversation. According to the moral, ethical guidelines set by your church, certain information cannot be shared without the patient's consent, which church leaders should adopt into their church protocol. More importantly, the interactions between the church and the deacon are important in that we understand how the deacon can be effective within the church as a church leader.

Chapter 5 said the deacon is often looked upon as a leader of the church, viewed as the go-to person in the church, and seen as a person of resource in the church. Knowing this, a deacon must maintain an agape love with the membership, showing empathy with the members' concerns and strength when they need an advocate in the community, always offering godly wisdom. With all those different attributes, you have to make sure you are staying within the understanding of your purpose of honest rapport, full of the Holy Ghost and wisdom. This is why training is so important when it comes to any leader, especially in the church, when you're dealing with the spiritual aspect of people's lives. We often see people at their worst, and we see people at their best, and during both times, we have to have the integrity and the trust of the membership, as well as those who walk through those doors of the local church.

Chapter 6 discusses the power of the deacon because with every leadership position, there's always someone in power. Consequently, the abuse of power may occur. As a result, I feel it is critical to address in this book, specifically when highlighting the importance of the deacon. I've found that integrity and honesty should always be at the forefront when it comes to ministry. Once you become a leader, your personal life becomes a public life, even in the church. In the eyes of church members, leaders, such as the pastor and deacon, are very significant. If you make one mistake, the congregation will hold you accountable for your actions. The relationship between the pastor and a deacon is vital in the preaching and teaching of the Gospel. If the pastor can rely on the deacon to care for the membership, then the pastor can spend more time in the word of God to bring forth a message for God's people. There is no place for division between the pastor and deacons. When there's division at the head of leadership, it affects the total membership body in a negative way, and then it extends outward into the community.

As chapter 7 said, the pastor/deacon relationship can be amazing when both parties respect each other. Deacons should see the pastor as a servant of God whose task is to teach and preach God's Word, equip and empower the saints, and spread the Word through missions. The pastor/deacon relationship should mimic the relationship Jesus had with His disciples. They ate together, walked together, and ministered together. When Jesus told the disciples to go out, they did. When He performed the miracle of feeding the multitude, it was the disciples who sat everyone down, passed out the food, and picked up the leftovers. They worked as a team, with Christ as the leader. But it was the leader Who washed their feet as He taught them about being humble and being a servant. And when Jesus ascended back into heaven, it was His disciples who were there, gathered together, watching Him go up. They were together up to the end.

This book, *7 Steps to Becoming an Acts 6 Deacon,* shows readers we believe in the peaceful union between the pastor and the deacon. I have been trained in both positions and realize the need for both to get along. Having a healthy and strong relationship with the pastor also helps encourage the pastor's sense of integrity in a loving way, because someone is walking alongside them, praying for them in the ministry, so they can share their concerns without reprisal.

I want to congratulate you for completing my book. I pray this book encourages you to make a strategic session phone call to begin your certification or continue your training to broaden your skill level as a deacon. If you are a pastor and choose to encourage your Deacon Board to attend the training, we can discuss that during a strategic session phone call too. All roads lead to www.JLWattsEnterprise.com for coaching and mentorship for pastors, deacons, and church leaders.

Endorsements

Pastor Watkins thoughtfully pens in **7 Steps to Becoming an Acts 6 Deacon** a framework of understanding that the **"ordination of a deacon is only the beginning"** of Christian service. There is a clear differentiation between the aspiration, the calling, the role, and the work of a deacon, and it is addressed in this work. Watkins uses the eleventh commandment of constructive criticism to prove that diaconate training should be reflective and continually revised **to serve this present age**. Psalm 33:11 states, **"The counsel of the Lord stands forever, the plans of His heart to all generations."** The biblical design for the work of deacons stands on its own and does not change, but the methodology of training must. Such training should thrust the deacon into a true parish ministry leadership role, supported by consistent Bible-based leadership training. This is courageous work. *7 Steps to Becoming an Acts 6 Deacon* will propel any diaconate for twenty-first-century ministry. May God be glorified.

Rev. Aaron Clewis
Pastor of Faith Community Church

I have been privileged to sit under your leadership and training both directly and indirectly, and without reservation, I can say my leadership proficiency has definitely been enhanced. Absolutely. Local (especially predominantly African-American) churches fall short in providing additional training postordination. There seems to be a major disinterest in investing in those we entrust with the leadership of our souls. This is a poor reflection on the understanding of scripture and its practical implications to not only honor leaders for their service but also to support them in their divinely delegated roles. Ongoing training helps to ensure trusted leaders are not only skillfully competent but also engaged in a spiritual formation process that helps to further undergird their personal holiness as well.

S.D. Hopkins, Pastor
Nazareth Baptist Church
Orange, VA

Deacons should continually be in training to be able to relate to a changing generation. For example, we have new viruses, and physicians must have continuous innovation and education. People come to our churches with issues that are not new but new to the church because the church pushed these issues under the rug or refused to acknowledge they existed. The church can no longer exist if these issues continue to be ignored. For example, mental illness and homosexuality are issues that exist, and deacons need to be able to minister to and serve these members effectively.

Professor Sophia Matthews
Biblical Leadership

Continuing education and training would be great because it would be more than just the surface. In the secular world, continuing education is a requirement in a number of occupations. As you said, the Bible does not change, God does not change, but people and life circumstances do. The pastor and deacon meet the people where they are.

Mrs. Ernestine Levette
Atlanta, GA

Questions

When you think of the deacons that you have known over the years, what names come to your mind?

Let's take this a step further. Does *your* name come up when others think of the deacon that made an impact on their lives?

Printed in the United States
by Baker & Taylor Publisher Services